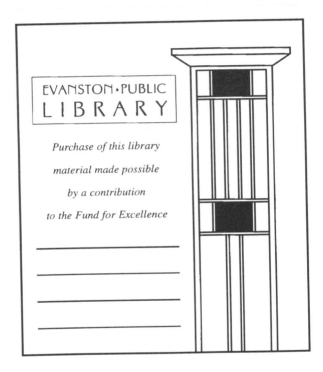

Learn to Say No!

Marijuana

Angela Royston

Heinemann Library
Chicago, Illinois

Designed by AMR
Illustrations by Art Construction
Originated by Ambassador
Printed in Hong Kong

04 03 02 01 00
10 9 8 7 6 5 4 3 2 1

Royston, Angela.
    Marijuana / Angela Royston.
      p. cm. – (Learn to say no!)
    Includes bibliographical references and index.
    Summary: Introduces marijuana—what it is, how it has been used, its effects on the body,
and the debate over legalization.
    ISBN 1-57572-238-0 (library binding)
      1. Marijuana—Juvenile literature. 2. Marijuana—Psychological aspects—Juvenile literature.
3. Marijuana—Physiological effect—Juvenile literature. 4. Drug abuse—Juvenile literature. 5.
Substance abuse—Prevention—Juvenile literature. [1. Marijuana. 2. Drug abuse.] I. Title.

HV5822.M3 R64 2000
362.29'5—dc21   99-088168

Acknowledgments
The Publishers would like to thank the following for permission to reproduce photographs:
Michael Brosilow, p. 29; Chris Honeywell, p. 15; Corbis/Dan Lamont, p. 7, p. 10; Corbis/Galen
Rowel, p. 11; Environmental Images/Dave Ellison, p. 4; Gareth Boden, pp. 22, 24, 26, 27; Image
Bank/Thierry Dosogne, p. 19; Image Bank/Peter Turner, p. 21; PhotoEdit/A. Ramey, p. 28; Rex
Features, pp. 18, 20; Science Photo Library/Mark De Fraeye, p. 6, p. 8; Science Photo
Library/Matt Meadows/Peter Arnold Inc. p. 17; Tony Stone/Simon Norfolk, pp. 5; Tony
Stone/David Roth, p. 23; Tony Stone/David Young Wolff, p. 25; Topham Pictures, p. 9.

Cover photograph reproduced with permission of Eye Ubiquitous and Tony Stone

Every effort has been made to contact copyright holders of any material reproduced in this
book. Any omissions will be rectified in subsequent printings if notice is given to the publisher.

Special thanks to Pam Richards for her help in the preparation of this book.

Some words are shown in bold, **like this.**
You can find out what they mean by looking in the glossary.

Contents

What Are Drugs?

A drug is any substance that affects your body and changes the way you feel. There are three groups of drugs—medicines, **legal drugs,** and **illegal drugs**.

Medicines

Many medicines, such as cough medicines and painkillers, help to soothe the symptoms of a disease. Other medicines, such as antiseptic cream and antibiotics, tackle the disease itself. Some medicines can only be **prescribed** by doctors, but over-the-counter medication can be bought at a drugstore or a grocery store.

Illegal or legal?

Legal drugs include medicines, of course, but the term usually refers to drugs such as alcohol and tobacco. These drugs affect the way a person feels, but they are not illegal for adults. Tea, coffee, and cola contain legal drugs, too. Illegal drugs include marijuana, **heroin**, Ecstasy, and **LSD**, and are forbidden by law.

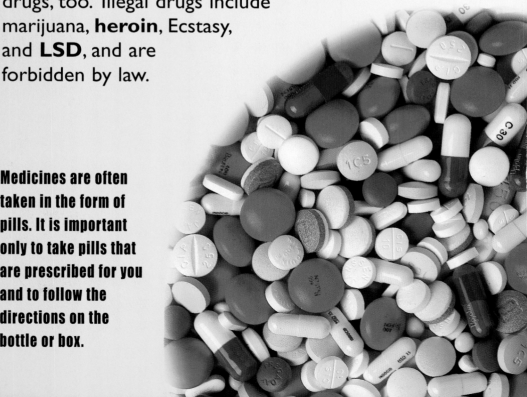

Medicines are often taken in the form of pills. It is important only to take pills that are prescribed for you and to follow the directions on the bottle or box.

 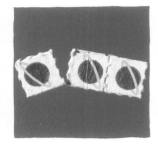 

These are all illegal drugs, which can be dangerous to take. They include stimulants and depressants— sometimes called **uppers** and **downers**—and hallucinogens.

Uppers and downers

Apart from medicines, most drugs are **stimulants**, **depressants,** or **hallucinogens**. A stimulant, such as caffeine, makes the body work faster. A depressant, such as alcohol, slows the body down and makes a person relax. A hallucinogen changes the way a person sees or hears things. Marijuana is both a depressant and a hallucinogen. This book tells about marijuana, what happens when people use it, and the dangers it causes.

Did you know?

There are many names for marijuana, and people are always making up new names for it. Names for marijuana include dope, weed, pot, reefer, hash, sinsemilla, ganja, **grass**, mary jane, herb, kif, wacky backy, skunk, and ganster.

What Is Marijuana?

Marijuana is made from a plant whose scientific name is *Cannabis sativa*. There are three forms of the drug cannabis, and each has a different name—**marijuana, hashish**, and hashish oil.

Hashish and marijuana
Hashish, or hash, is a hard, brownish-black block. It is made by drying the whole plant and then rubbing it to make the **resin** into hashish. Some hashish is stronger than other hashish, depending mainly on where the plant was grown. Marijuana is also called **grass** or weed. It is made from the green or gray leaves and stalks, which are dried and chopped. Marijuana is the most often used illegal drug in the United States.

Sinsemilla and Hashish oil
Sinsemilla is made from the male flowers of the plant and is stronger than most forms of hash. Hashish oil is made from the juice. There is debate as to whether it should be allowed to be legally **prescribed** as a medicine for **multiple sclerosis** and other diseases. **THC**, a prescription drug made from marijuana, may be given to lessen the unpleasant side effects of **chemotherapy**.

Cannabis is a kind of hemp and grows easily in most parts of the world. Every part of the plant can be made into the drug.

These special pipes are called hash pipes. Hash or grass is placed in the bowl and smoked. Most users, however, roll the drugs up to make a joint.

How marijuana is used

Marijuana is usually smoked. Grass and hash are rolled into a **joint** or smoked in a pipe. In some cases, grass is smoked with tobacco to make a very less powerful joint.

Did you know?

Marijuana contains more than 400 different chemicals. When it is smoked, it produces more than 2,000 chemicals, which are breathed into the lungs. Many of these chemicals damage the lungs and other parts of the body.

Which is true?

It is said that during the Crusades, Muslim fighters were given hashish before being sent off to kill Christians. Today, people say the opposite—that marijuana makes people feel relaxed and more sympathetic to those around them. Do you think that both views could be true, depending on the circumstances?

A Mixed History

People have been using marijuana for thousands of years. They used it not only for pleasure, but also as a medicine. A Chinese book of remedies collected for Emperor Shen Nung included it nearly 5,000 years ago. The drug then spread to India, and by the 1840s, doctors in the West began to use it, too. In England, Queen Victoria's favorite doctor treated many illnesses and complaints with marijuana.

Chinese medicines use many kinds of herbs and other things, such as sliced horn. The herbs are weighed and put into plastic bags ready for use.

Increase in popularity

In 1937, the United States government made possessing or selling marijuana a crime. But in spite of the laws, the drug became very popular during the 1960s and 1970s. Many young people in Europe, North America, and Australia began to smoke marijuana regularly. It became the most commonly used illegal drug and the second most commonly used drug, with alcohol being the first.

In the 1970s, a survey estimated that 43 million Americans—nearly 20 percent of the population—had tried marijuana. Today, it is estimated that more than 70 million Americans over the age of 12 have tried it at least once.

Declining popularity

However, a 1999 study conducted by the U.S. Department of Human Services shows that drug use among teenagers declined or stayed at the same level for the three consecutive years of 1997, 1998, and 1999.

Other studies also show that the number of regular marijuana users has decreased by 40 percent since 1985, and that 86 percent of 12- to 17- year-olds have never tried marijuana.

In the 1960s, many young people began to smoke marijuana. It became part of a "hippie" way of life that included a particular style of music and clothes.

Think about it

Many people who were hippies in the 1960s and 1970s look back on that time as an exciting and idealistic age. Other people say that hippies only remember the good things and forget the problems and difficulties. What do you think?

Marijuana and the Law

Possession

Marijuana is an **illegal drug**. It is against the law to have it in your **possession**, for example in your pocket, among your belongings, or at home. When people smoke marijuana, they usually make a **joint** and pass it from one to the other, each taking a puff. Everyone who holds the joint is legally guilty of possession.

Marijuana is an illegal substance along with crack **cocaine** and **methamphetamine**. Punishment for possession of any of these illegal drugs depends on where the offender is caught. But one thing is for sure, the penalties for possession can include high fines and time in jail.

The police seize tons of drugs every year. About 80 percent is marijuana.

Drug dealing

Selling or supplying drugs is a much more serious offense. This is known as **drug dealing**. Dealing includes giving marijuana to others, even as a gift. If someone is caught with a large quantity of marijuana, the police assume that they are a dealer and will arrest them, particularly if the marijuana is divided into several smaller amounts.

In the United States, the penalty for dealing in marijuana for the first offense is up to five years in prison or a fine of up to $250,000. The situation in other countries varies. In some countries, such as Thailand, the penalties for possessing and dealing in marijuana can be much more severe.

Smuggling drugs is a very serious offense. This specially trained drug-sniffing dog can smell drugs on people and in luggage.

Marijuana and crime

According to the United States Drug Enforcement Administration (DEA) the U.S. government took $86 million worth of marijuana away from dealers in 1998.

In big U.S. cities, an average of 38 percent of the adult males arrested in 1998 were high on marijuana at the time of their arrest.

Did you know?

In 1998, over 700,000 people were arrested for possession of illegal drugs. The highest rates of arrest were in Washington, New Jersey, and New York. Today, the United States spends $27 billion each year to prevent drug abuse.

What Happens When Marijuana Is Smoked?

Lung damage

When someone smokes marijuana, the smoke goes down the **trachea** and into the lungs. The smoke from marijuana is very hot. It burns the throat and damages the delicate lining of the lungs. Some people hold the smoke in their mouth to let it cool before breathing it in. In the lungs, chemicals from the marijuana and any tobacco in the **joint** pass into the blood and are pumped all around the body.

Poisonous chemicals

The main chemical in marijuana that affects the brain the most is Tetrahydrocannabinol, called **THC**. Marijuana also contains many chemicals present in tobacco in a more concentrated form. It also contains more **tar** than tobacco. Tar collects in the lungs and can cause **cancer**. Marijuana, like tobacco, contains hydrogen cyanide—a deadly poison—ammonia, and carbon monoxide. Carbon monoxide reduces the amount of oxygen in the blood and damages the heart. Joints that have tobacco also contain nicotine, a very **addictive** chemical.

Smoking marijuana affects the body in a few minutes and lasts from three to five hours. The diagram shows some of the physical effects.

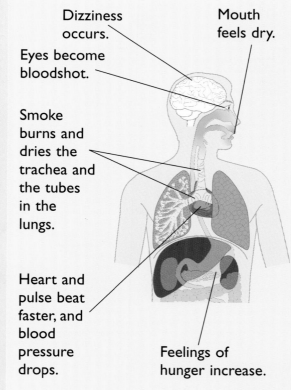

Dizziness occurs.

Mouth feels dry.

Eyes become bloodshot.

Smoke burns and dries the trachea and the tubes in the lungs.

Heart and pulse beat faster, and blood pressure drops.

Feelings of hunger increase.

Eating marijuana

When marijuana is cooked and eaten, the drug passes through the stomach and is digested into the blood. It begins to affect the body about an hour after it is swallowed. Eating marijuana may avoid the hazards of smoking, but the main problem is that it is harder to control the amount taken. Once swallowed, it cannot be **diluted**.

Varying strengths

The strength of this drug is measured by the amount of THC. Most marijuana has about three to four percent THC. **Hashish** has from ten to fifteen percent THC, which is about five to eight times the amount of THC as marijuana. Hashish oil contains nearly 70 percent THC. Single joints can also vary in strength, depending on how much marijuana is used.

Did you know?

Cannabis is a form of **hemp,** a plant that is made into rope, twine, canvas, and clothes. Hemp is produced in many countries in the world, including the United States, but it is grown mainly in parts of North Africa, the Near East, and southern Asia.

A cigarette made with marijuana is called a joint. A joint contains more cancer-causing chemicals than a tobacco cigarette.

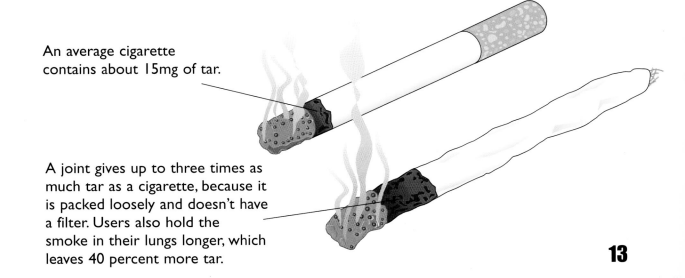

An average cigarette contains about 15mg of tar.

A joint gives up to three times as much tar as a cigarette, because it is packed loosely and doesn't have a filter. Users also hold the smoke in their lungs longer, which leaves 40 percent more tar.

The Effects of Smoking Marijuana

The effects of smoking marijuana are not very obvious, particularly at first. A person may smoke several times before he or she notices any effect at all. Even then, the person may only notice talking and laughing a lot, but not realize that it is due to the marijuana.

Stoned
A person is said to be **stoned** when they are clearly affected by marijuana. Sounds and other sensations become more noticable. Some people become talkative, while others become lethargic and withdrawn.

Some people feel "in tune" with what they are doing. They may feel that they are playing an instrument unusually well, for example. In fact, people who are stoned perform less well at all tasks. The illusion of performing well is particularly dangerous for anyone who is driving a car. Marijuana affects judgement and coordination, both of which are very important when driving a vehicle.

Think about it
Marijuana affects a person's sense of time, memory, balance, and coordination. What sort of problems could this lead to? Imagine, for example, if someone walked home after a party before the effects of marijuana had worn off.

Depression and anxiety

Marijuana can cause many unpleasant feelings. A person's experience of marijuana will be affected by his or her mood. Some people may feel relaxed and sympathetic to people around them. But if they are depressed, marijuana can make them more depressed. Some people become anxious and may panic, particularly if they are not used to the drug. If a lot of marijuana is taken, the person loses track of time and may become forgetful and confused. Stoned people are more likely to have accidents because balance and coordination are greatly affected.

Marijuana makes colors more intense and shapes sharper. In the 1960s, patterns like this were called psychedelic and were often designed by people who liked the effects of marijuana and LSD.

15

Frequent Use and Its Effects

Effects on the body

Marijuana is not physically **addictive**. This means that although people may smoke it regularly and heavily, their bodies do not need it to function normally. Unlike an alcoholic, who has to drink increasing amounts to get drunk, a marijuana user does not need to smoke more to become **stoned**.

However, marijuana is harmful to the body. Marijuana contains many **chemicals** that cause **cancer** of the lungs, throat, and neck. Tobacco also contains cancer-causing chemicals, and it is thought that marijuana may increase the deadly effects of tobacco. Marijuana increases the problems of heart disease, such as hypertension and hardening of the arteries.

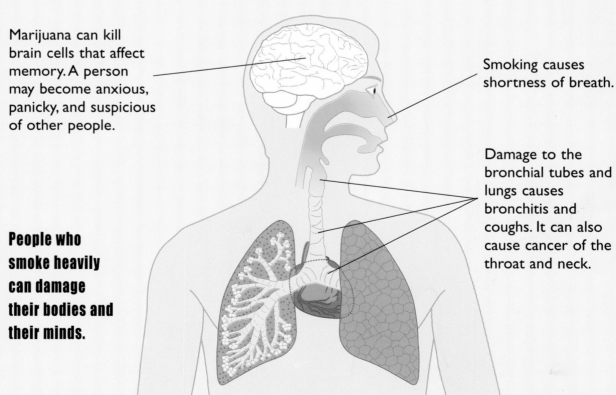

Marijuana can kill brain cells that affect memory. A person may become anxious, panicky, and suspicious of other people.

Smoking causes shortness of breath.

Damage to the bronchial tubes and lungs causes bronchitis and coughs. It can also cause cancer of the throat and neck.

People who smoke heavily can damage their bodies and their minds.

Unborn babies

Pregnant women who regularly smoke marijuana may affect their babies. When the mother takes marijuana into her body, some of it passes through to her unborn baby. For several months after it is born, the marijuana in the baby's body may cause it to shake, be easily startled, and be distressed. Babies whose mothers regularly use marijuana are more likely to be born **prematurely**.

Marijuana is sometimes mixed with tobacco when it is smoked. Marijuana and tobacco both damage lungs and can cause diseases, such as lung cancer. These are the dirty and damaged lungs of a smoker.

Assessing research

Scientists do not agree on how harmful marijuana is. Some studies say that it harms the parts of the brain that control memory and emotion, and weakens the white blood cells that protect against disease. The THC from marijuana can stay in the body, interrupting the brain cells' ability to send and read signals, and attacking white blood cells, for up to a month.

The Social Effects

Addiction

Marijuana is not physically **addictive,** but it can be psychologically addictive. This means that some people rely on it to feel happy and sociable. The effects of a **joint** can last for several hours, so by smoking two or three joints a day, people can be **stoned** most of the time. When they are not stoned, they may be very bad tempered, and some people become **paranoid**.

Losing touch

Heavy smokers of marijuana lose their motivation. They tend to spend most of the time sitting around and not getting on with their lives. They may have big plans, but they do not put them into action. Students might not work hard and may fail their tests at school. People who are stoned most of the time become cut off from their families and their work. They become isolated and lonely. This can make them smoke even more.

Being stoned most of the time stops people from living their lives. They may have big plans, but do nothing to put them into action.

18

Crime

Marijuana is expensive, so heavy smokers have to find a way to pay for it. Some turn to crime, such as stealing, so that they can sell the stolen items for money. People who buy marijuana from **drug dealers** are in danger of getting involved in crime, too. If they buy marijuana for their friends as well and are caught, they will be accused of drug dealing. Dealers are criminals who may also deal in **heroin, LSD,** and other dangerous drugs. They often frighten their customers and try to make them buy other drugs. Some dealers let first time customers have the drugs supposedly free on approval. However, the dealers soon want their money. The users often can't afford to pay the dealers, so they turn to crime.

Most people who use heroin and other dangerous drugs began by smoking marijuana. But most marijuana users do not go on to use other drugs.

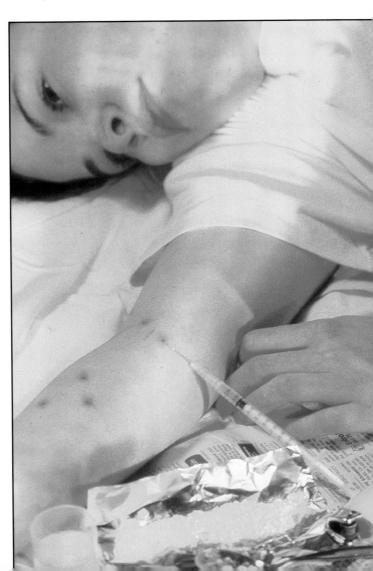

Did you know?

A quarter of an ounce (seven grams) of marijuana costs about the same as two videotapes or two CDs. For the price of half an ounce (fourteen grams) of marijuana, you could buy an expensive pair of shoes or some clothes.

Why Do Some People Do It?

Following the crowd?

Some people use marijuana because it helps them feel more confident and less shy. As **joints** are usually passed around, with each person taking one puff at a time, marijuana can give people a false feeling of sharing and friendliness. But these are not true feelings. You can be yourself and have good friends without marijuana.

Most people first try marijuana because they are curious about it and because others are trying it. But it is important to think for yourself and not harm your health or become involved in an illegal activity.

People often think that outdoor festivals are safe and legal places to take drugs. But drugs are unsafe and illegal at festivals, just as they are everywhere else.

Marijuana mystique

Marijuana is illegal and can be harmful. Some young people find it exciting to break the law and defy their parents and teachers by smoking it. It makes them feel independent and cool.

Smoking marijuana gives people the feeling that they know about something that ordinary people don't know about. Others try to show how cool they are by talking about how **stoned** they have been. But don't believe everything that people say about being stoned. Some people exaggerate the effects, because they do not want to admit that they did not feel much of anything.

Marijuana has a strong smell. People who smoke it sometimes burn incense to cover the smell. The odor of drugs or the smell of incense or other cover-up scents can be signs that someone you know is using drugs.

Did you know?

Marijuana use is not just an urban problem. A study published in 2000 by the Center on Addiction and Substance Abuse found that eighth-graders in rural areas are 34 percent more likely to smoke marijuana than eighth-graders in urban centers.

Money well spent?

Do you think governments should spend large sums of money trying to prevent people from taking drugs? How would you dissuade people from taking drugs?

Saying No

What will you do if your friends start to smoke marijuana or if you are offered a **joint**? Many people are worried that if they say no, their friends will think they are stupid and childish. But it is more mature to be able to say you don't want to smoke than to smoke when you don't want to.

Reasons for saying no

This book gives you plenty of reasons for saying no, such as "It's illegal!" You can think of other possible things that you might say, such as "I don't want a criminal record," or "I have homework to do." But you really don't have to give an excuse.

You don't need to use marijuana to have fun. These friends enjoy being together without smoking, drinking, or using drugs.

What you say matters less than how you say it. Clearly say that you don't want any marijuana. Friends or people who offer you marijuana are more likely to try to persuade you if they sense that you are uncertain. Remember, marijuana is an **illegal drug.**

Life without marijuana

You do not need to smoke marijuana to have a relaxed and enjoyable time with your friends. You can listen to music and talk without getting **stoned**—and you won't be breaking the law.

Did you know?

Most people have not tried marijuana. More than 200 million Americans have never smoked marijuana.

Working hard at school and doing your homework will help you to be successful when you finish school. Smoking marijuana causes some students to lose interest in school.

Dealing with Difficult Situations

Avoid situations in which you might be asked to try marijuana. For example, if you suspect that your friends are going to someone's house to smoke marijuana, it is better to not go than to go and refuse to join in. If you find yourself in a situation where people are smoking a **joint**, don't panic! Leave the area or call an adult to pick you up.

Finding new friends

If your friends are experimenting with marijuana, alcohol, or other illegal and harmful things, you should think about whether they are the best friends for you.

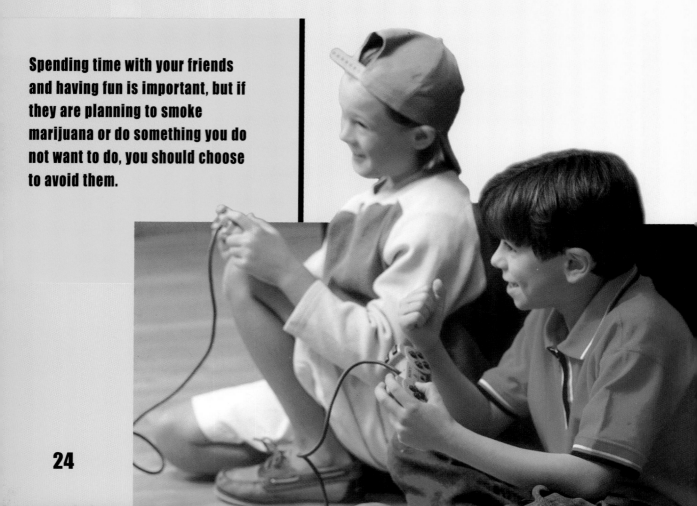

Spending time with your friends and having fun is important, but if they are planning to smoke marijuana or do something you do not want to do, you should choose to avoid them.

Friendships are important, and it is not always easy to change friends. But you can try to spend more time with other people. You could join a club or play on a team at a local sports center. Exercise not only keeps you fit, but it makes you feel good. If you are stressed or anxious, you will feel more relaxed and calm after doing aerobics or swimming for half an hour, than after smoking a joint.

The pressures of life

Hard work, tests at school, and pressure from parents or friends can cause stress. Can using marijuana help a person who feels stressed, or would it just lead to more problems?

Did you know?

Most people who try marijuana do not go on to use it regularly. Researchers have found that marijuana use declines after people reach their late teens and early twenties.

There are plenty of clubs and activities that you can do after school. You will make new friends, too.

Growing Up

Changing friends

As you grow up, you become more independent of your family. Being in a group with your friends can seem very important. You might want to be friends with the most exciting people in the class, but it is better to choose friends that you like and who like the same kinds of things as you. Part of growing up is finding out who you are. You may change your group of friends several times as you grow older and discover more about yourself.

The music you listen to and the clothes you like to wear say a lot about who you are. You don't need to smoke marijuana, too.

Good and bad times

Growing up is an exciting and enjoyable time. You can try out new things and begin to make decisions for yourself. It can also be a difficult time. There are important tests to take. Friendships won't always run smoothly. Most young people worry about the way they look, whether people will like them, and what they are going to do with their lives.

Getting help

Some young people have serious problems at home or at school. If you have problems that you feel you cannot deal with, don't despair. Ask for help. There are people and organizations who can help you. If you can, ask for help from your family, your friends, or your teachers. If at first people don't listen to you, keep looking and asking for help until you get it.

Did you know?

Marijuana Anonymous is an organization in the U.S. that provides help and support for people who want to stop using marijuana. The telephone number is (800) 766-6779.

Talking about a problem can help you feel better or help you to find a solution. If you can't talk to a friend or someone in your family, talk to an adult you can trust, such as a teacher.

Not Prescribed, Not Approved

Marijuana as medicine?

There are some people who say that marijuana can have a medical use for certain illnesses and conditions. However, since 1970, United States law has classified marijuana as a Schedule I controlled substance. This means that smoking marijuana is not accepted for medical use.

The chemical **THC**, which is found in marijuana, is made into a pill form. It is a prescription drug and can only be **prescribed** by a doctor. It is prescribed for **cancer** patients to treat the symptoms of nausea and vomiting that can occur with certain cancer treatments. THC can also be prescribed for severely ill **AIDS** patients to help them eat more and to keep up their weight.

Scientists agree that much more research needs to be done to discover the side effects and possible benefits of marijuana. At this time, smoking marijuana has no regular medical use.

Doctors in the United States can prescribe pills containing THC, the active ingredient in marijuana. Smoking marijuana is never prescribed.

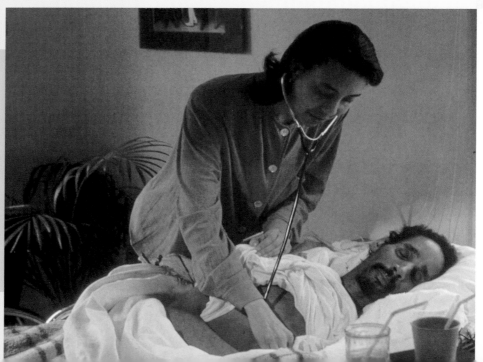

Quality control

There is no way of knowing the quality of an illegal drug, such a marijuana. It might be dangerously impure or it might be mixed with harmless tea leaves. Legal drugs receive Food and Drug Administration (FDA) approval. This agency of the U.S. Department of Health and Human Services oversees the safety of legal drugs.

Is it tea leaves, marijuana, or something even more dangerous? With an illegal drug, you can never be sure.

Did you know?

Marijuana intoxication negatively affects the brain. It impairs reading comprehension, memory, speech, the ability to solve problems, and reaction time.

Talking point

Medical research indicates that the drug in marijuana, THC, relieves symptoms of glaucoma, an eye disease. It is also said to relieve nausea caused by chemotherapy and radiation treatments. What position do you think the medical community should take regarding THC?

Useful Contacts

Marijuana

Marijuana Anonymous – offers confidential support to people who want to stop using marijuana:
telephone: (800) 766-6779.

Other Problems

Covenant House – talk to a counselor about problems with friends, family, schol, drugs, or alcohol:
telephone: (800) 999-9999.

Drug and Alcohol Abuse Hotline– for counseling:
telephone: (800) 729-6686.

Spanish Hotline – talk to a counselor in Spanish about drugs and alcohol:
telephone: (800) 344-7432.

More Books to Read

Desmond, Theresa, and Paul Almonte. *Drug Use and Abuse*. Parsippany, N.J.: Silver Burdett Press, 1995.

Jaffe, Steven L. *How to Get Help*. Broomall, Penn.: Chelsea House Publishers, 1999.

Sanders, Pete, and Steve Myers. *Drugs*. Brookfield, Conn.: Millbrook Press, Inc., 1996.

Marijuana. Broomall, Penn.: Chelsea House, 1999.

Glossary

AIDS disease that damages the body's ability to fight disease

addictive causing someone to form a habit they cannot give up

cancer serious illness in which new cells in part of the body grow uncontrollably

chemotherapy treatment of cancer using strong drugs that poison the cancer

cocaine illegal drug that is a stimulant

depressant substance that slows down the body's reactions and relaxes the muscles

dilute make weaker by the addition of water or another liquid

downer another word for a depressant

drug dealing selling drugs

grass slang name for marijuana

hallucinogen drug that heightens experiences or makes things that are imagined seem real

hashish brownish-black block made from the whole marijuana plant

hemp plant family to which marijuana belongs

heroin addictive, illegal drug made from a particular kind of poppy

illegal drug drug, such as heroin, LSD, or marijuana, which is forbidden by law

joint cigarette made from marijuana or from marijuana mixed with tobacco

legal drug substance that affects the body but is allowed by law, such as medicines, coffee, and tea

LSD illegal, powerful hallucinogen

methamphetamine white or slightly yellow crystal-like powder that comes in rock-like chunks

multiple sclerosis disease of the spinal cord and the brain that affects the muscles and causes difficulties with speech

paranoid feeling persecuted without real cause

possession something held or owned

prematurely too early

prescribed given a medicine under the advice or order of a doctor

resin sticky juice that flows from certain plants and trees

stimulant substance that speeds up the body

stoned strongly affected by marijuana

tar thick, black, sticky substance made by burning tobacco

THC chemical in marijuana that produces relaxation and hallucinations

trachea windpipe. It carries air to the lungs.

upper stimulant

Index